Mini Cushions
IN CROSS STITCH

x x x x x x x x x x x x x x x x x x x

Mini Cushions

IN CROSS STITCH

x x x x x x x x x x x x x x x x x

Sheena Rogers

GUILD OF MASTER
CRAFTSMAN PUBLICATIONS

First published 2006 by
Guild of Master Craftsman Publications Ltd,
166 High Street, Lewes,
East Sussex BN7 1XU

Production Manager: Hilary MacCallum
Managing Editor: Gerrie Purcell
Editor: Rachel Netherwood
Photography: Anthony Bailey
Managing Art Editor: Gilda Pacitti
Design: Maggie Aldred

Typefaces: Weiss, Flemish Script

Colour origination: Wyndeham Graphics
Printed and bound: Hing Yip Printing Co. Ltd

Measurements notice

Imperial measurements are conversions from metric; they have been rounded
up or down to the nearest $\frac{1}{4}$, $\frac{1}{2}$ or whole inch. When following the projects,
use either the metric or the imperial measurements; do not mix units.

Contents

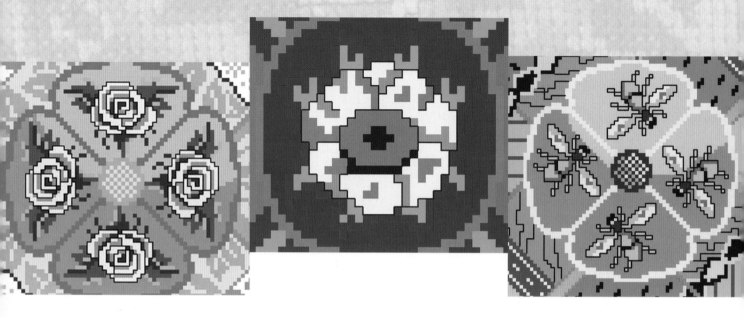

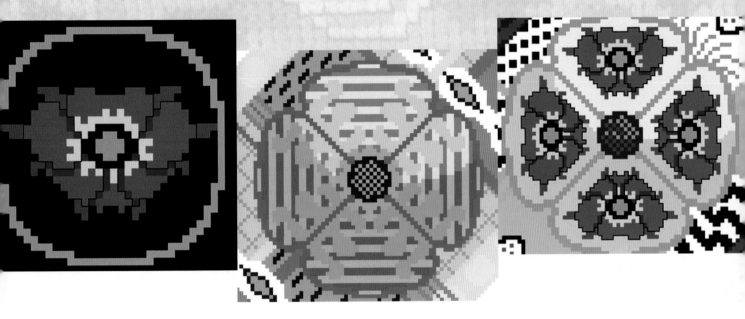

Introduction

All of the designs featured in this book were created using the template of a large four-petal flower within a square of colourful patchwork patterns. A myriad of these patterns and colours have been combined to create a cluster of sumptuous cushions with which to decorate your home, give as presents or to frame as pictures, but mostly just for you to enjoy. At the back of this book you will find a blank template for you to design your own unique cushion, so let your imagination run wild and have fun experimenting with colour and texture combinations. Enjoy exploring these vivid designs and along your journey you will discover all the techniques you need to create your own cluster of cushions, including cross stitch, back stitch, beading and tweeding.

The designs in this book are charted onto a grid of small squares. Each of these small squares contains a symbol that represents one stitch on a piece of fabric. As these designs were stitched using the technique called 'cross stitch', one square on the chart would result in one cross on the fabric. Where beads have been attached to some of the designs, this is again represented on the chart with one square equalling one bead.

The Projects

Plants and Nature

Poppy Precious

Wild Thistle

Blue Posy

Daisy Daisy

*Daisy Daisy Card
and Honeypot Cover*

Twilight Fantasy

Twilight Fantasy Card

Orange Blossom

Orchid Delight

Beautiful Bugs

Flutterflies

Fossil Frenzy

Swirling Shells

Tropical Forest

Rusty Leaves

Poppy Precious

Bright red poppies fill this design, surrounded with bold black and white patterns, which are interspersed with blocks of solid colours. The white areas are formed by leaving patches of the Aida fabric unstitched, making this a relatively quick design to stitch.

To add a rich texture to this mini cushion, try replacing the red stitches with shiny red seed beads to create poppies that will jump out of the design. But if you prefer a cooler feel to your stitching, replace the light and dark shades of cream thread with icy blue shades.

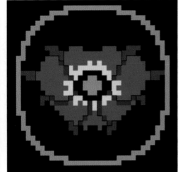

Colour variations for Poppy Precious

Poppy Precious

		DMC	ANCHOR	MADEIRA
		Cross stitch in 2 strands		
	■	310	Black	Black
	◩	321	47	0510
	+	414	235	1801
	★	677	886	2207
	◆◆	742	303	0107
	♡	746	275	0101
	▼	814	45	0514
	✒	841	1082	1911
	▪▪	904	258	1413
	✕	918	341	0314
	✳	3031	1088	2003
	▼	3708	31	0408
	•	3845	1089	1103
		Back stitch in 1 strand		
═	──	310	Black	Black

Wild Thistle

*T*his design uses dusty shades of pinks, creams and greys to create a harsh yet beautiful wilderness. The darker shades of green, brown and yellow give an earthy quality to the design – ideal colours for creating a country setting.

Beads and back stitching also feature in this design, so starting in the middle of your fabric and at the centre of the chart, work all of the cross stitching first, then use the dark grey thread to complete the back stitching. Lastly, add the beads to the centre of the design and your stitching is ready to be made up into a mini cushion or framed as a picture. Try incorporating other ideas into the design, such as using seed beads for the blue thistles, or replacing the shades of cream thread with powder green shades to give the design a spring-like feel.

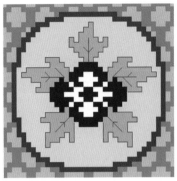

Colour variations for Wild Thistle

Wild Thistle

		DMC	ANCHOR	MADEIRA
		Cross stitch in 2 strands		
	+	151	73	0607
	▼	168	1037	1001
	•	340	1030	0902
	◖	413	400	1713
	=	413+168	400+1037	1713+1001
	♥	498	1006	0511
	★	677	886	2207
	▽	743	305	0113
	$	746	275	0101
	■	791	123	0904
	⊠	801	359	2007
	••	3045	888	2103
	✳	3345	263	1405
	⊖	3609	85	0710
	◆◆	3731	77	0610
	◆	Blanc	2	White
		Back stitch in 1 strand		
	—	413	400	1713
	B	Lilac blue beads		
	■	Dark blue beads		

Blue Posy

Small sprigs of blue flowers and buds are the main theme within this design. For a fresh spring look, try using the blue shades of thread in place of the brown, red and pink shades that feature in the 'patchwork' background.

Beads have been added in the centre of the design and you could extend their use by replacing the light and dark blue shades of stranded cotton within the flowers with light and dark blue seed beads to create a glistening raised effect.

One of the small sprig motifs could be used to create a delightful matching card. Try experimenting with various combinations of thread colour to create a collection of cards that each feature a different coloured flower.

Mini Cushions in Cross Stitch

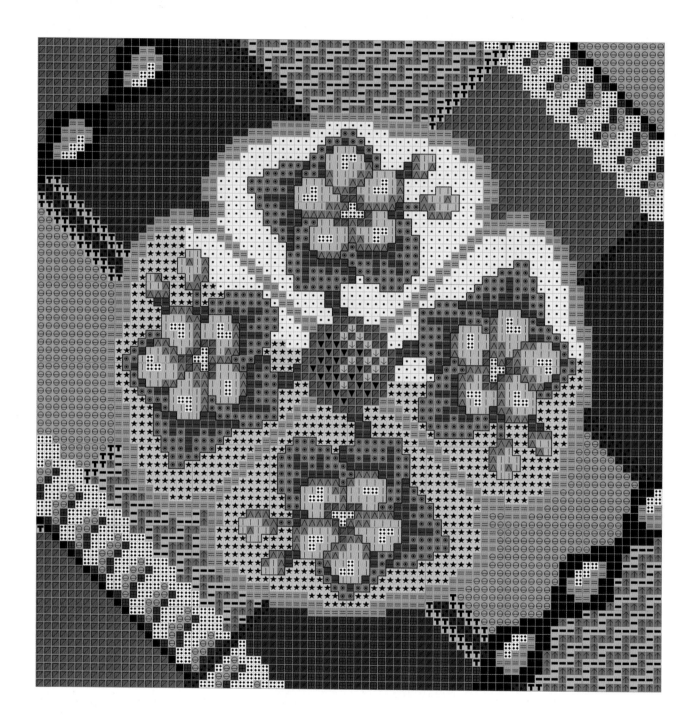

Colour variation
for Blue Posy

Blue Posy

		DMC	ANCHOR	MADEIRA
		Cross stitch in 2 strands		
	∧	322	978	1004
	◉	368	214	1310
	=	436	1045	2011
	■	452	232	1807
	↑	517	162	1107
	◩	632	371	2304
	★	745	301	0111
	•	746	275	0101
	⊖	760	1022	0405
	■	791	123	0904
			794	121	0907
	T	973	290	0105
	▬	986	246	1313
	■	3031	1088	2003
	✕	3041	871	0806
	⊞	3777	1015	0407
	⠿	Blanc	2	White
		Back stitch in 1 strand		
	—	3031	1088	2003
	↓	Light blue beads		
	▼	Dark blue beads		

Daisy Daisy

This design conjures up the image of sitting down to a picnic in a lush green meadow peppered with delicate daisies on a glorious summer's day as bees, heavy with pollen, float by in the hazy sunshine.

Some of the crisp white Aida fabric has been left unstitched, making this a fairly quick design to complete. If you have more time, try filling the white patches with powder blue cross stitches for that added touch of clear summer skies.

A new design could be created by moving the bees into the four large petal shapes and stitching a daisy in each corner of the design. Use the blank template on page 172 to help you plot the stitches.

Daisy Daisy

*Design variation
for Daisy Daisy*

Daisy Daisy Cushion

		DMC	ANCHOR	MADEIRA
		Cross stitch in 2 strands		
	■	310	Black	Black
	↑	444	291	0105
	│	564	206	1208
	⊞	699	230	1303
	◉	801	359	2007
	T	817	46	0211
	▶	817+Blanc	46+2	0211+White
	◆	927	849	1708
	⊞	992	1072	1202
	—	3822	305	0109
	▬	3823	386	0111
	●	3829	901	2212
	∧	Blanc	2	White
		Back stitch in 1 strand		
	▬	310	Black	Black
	—	817	46	0211

Daisy Daisy Card and Honeypot Cover

x x x x x x x x x x x x x x x x x x

The colours and motifs that appear in the Daisy Daisy mini cushion have been gathered together to form this matching card design. For a different effect, try replacing the dark cream cross stitches with pale, sky blue thread.

This versatile design is not just limited to a card: cut a piece of Aida fabric approximately 7in (180mm) square and fray each edge for about ½in (12mm). Then cross stitch this design in the centre of the fabric but omit the red and brown border. This will make a delightful topper for a jar of honey or jam and can be fastened in place by tying a piece of green or red ribbon around the rim of the jar.

See 'Making up a Greetings Card' on page 170

Daisy Daisy Card and Honeypot Cover

		DMC	ANCHOR	MADEIRA
		Cross stitch in 2 strands		
■	■	310	Black	Black
■	↑	444	291	0105
■	│	564	206	1208
■	▣	699	230	1303
■	◉	801	359	2007
■	◆	817	46	0211
■	◆	927	849	1708
■	⊞	992	1072	1202
■	—	3822	305	0109
■	●	3829	901	2212
■	∧	Blanc	2	White
		Back stitch in 1 strand		
▦	—	310	Black	Black
▦	—	817	46	0211

Twilight Fantasy

Warm, bold and sultry colours from the East appear in this design inspired by animal prints and tropical flowers. Lime green beads add sparkle and texture to the centre of each delicate flower. The use of white across both the patchwork background and the flowers brings the whole design together.

To create a mini cushion that will coordinate with your decor, try replacing the yellow, pink and red stitches with threads that match the colours in your own home furnishings.

Replacing the white stitches with shiny white seed beads will add even more texture to the finished piece.

Design variation for Twilight Fantasy

Twilight Fantasy Cushion

		DMC	ANCHOR	MADEIRA
		Cross stitch in 2 strands		
	■	310	Black	Black
	✹	414	235	1801
	✳	505	210	1213
	◥	718	88	0707
	▥	815	44	0513
	✚	973	290	0105
	▽	3042	870	0807
	◪	3834	100	0713
	▼	3835	97	0711
	✗	3841	1031	1001
	⊖	Blanc	2	White
		Back stitch in 1 strand		
	—	310	Black	Black
	★	Lime green beads		

Twilight Fantasy Card

x x x x x x x x x x x x x x x x x x x x x

Where lime green beads were used in the mini cushion design, lime green stranded cotton has been used in this card design which gives the finished piece a subtle effect. For a bolder card, replace the striped background with single black cross stitches, stitched at random on the unstitched white fabric. This will make the design even quicker to complete if you are short on time.

To make a larger cushion for your home, stitch the mini cushion design onto a piece of Aida fabric approximately 15in (380mm) square, then stitch the card design in each of the four corners. Extend the yellow, black and pink stripes across the top, bottom and sides to link up the four designs.

See 'Making up a Greetings Card' on page 170

Twilight Fantasy Card

		DMC	ANCHOR	MADEIRA
		Cross stitch in 2 strands		
	■	310	Black	Black
	✳	505	210	1213
	★	704	256	1308
	◩	718	88	0707
	+	973	290	0105
	▽	3042	870	0807
	●	3834	100	0713
	▼	3835	97	0711
	⊖	Blanc	2	White
		Back stitch in 1 strand		
	——	310	Black	Black

Orange Blossom

Sweet, scented blossom in early spring can soon be blown away on the lightest of breezes, but this mini cushion design has captured the essence of this blossom for all time. Fiery orange and red threads have been chosen for stitching the blossom in a contemporary style but they can be easily replaced with crisp white and palest pink shades of stranded cotton for a more traditional image of blossom.

The brown stripy pattern and diagonal lines cutting across the design represent a garden trellis or fence, adding a 'woody' feel. The small blossom motif could also be stitched to make a matching greetings card, by surrounding it with pale blue cross stitches.

Colour variation for Orange Blossom

Orange Blossom

	DMC	ANCHOR	MADEIRA
Cross stitch in 2 strands			
■	336	149	1007
△	402	1047	2307
▣	414	235	1801
←	677	886	2207
○	754	1012	0305
⬇	801	359	2007
▽	841	1082	1911
⊖	869	375	2105
⊞	3042	870	0807
⊥	3778	1013	2310
▬	3801	29	0411
+	3840	120	0907
÷	Blanc	2	White
Back stitch in 1 strand			
——	310	Black	Black

Orchid Delight

$\mathcal{D}$elicate pink orchids fill this design surrounded by a mix of warm, tropical colours and cool seaside stripes. Seed beads have been added to create a swirling green pattern in opposite corners. They are also used to spell the word 'Orchid' which adds more interest to an otherwise regular, geometric design.

Other colour combinations could be experimented with, such as cross stitching pale cream orchids surrounded by powder green stitches, or bright yellow orchids with a pale pink surround. Try changing the colour of the beads to match the orchid colours. Bright pink, purple or blue seed beads will look equally attractive surrounded by the stranded cotton shades that have been used in this design.

Colour variations for Orchid Delight

Orchid Delight

		DMC	ANCHOR	MADEIRA
		Cross stitch in 2 strands		
	∧	153	103	0801
	T	162	1031	1001
	▶	350	11	0213
	▮	699	230	1303
	⊞	826	977	1012
	◆	932	343	1710
	▬	951	1009	2308
	⊖	977	1002	2307
	■	3031	1088	2003
	—	3364	260	1603
	◺	3607	87	0708
	✖	3608	86	0709
	≡	3768	779	1706
		Back stitch in 1 strand		
	——	3031	1088	2003
	▮	Dark green beads		

Beautiful Bugs

*F*our beautiful bugs have been repeated at different angles to form the theme of this mini cushion. Earthy colours are combined with shades of blue to give an outdoor feel to the design. The small brown blocks of cross stitches appear as small insects against the size of the four main bugs and the back stitched geometric lines are an interpretation of the networks of tunnels built by ants underground.

The wings of the bugs could be stitched with shiny metallic threads to catch the light and different shades of green threads could be used within the patterned background to give the design a warm summer feel.

This design would look equally attractive mounted in a pine wood frame and hung on a kitchen wall.

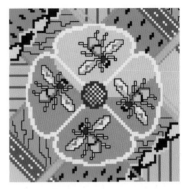

Colour variation for Beautiful Bugs

Beautiful Bugs

		DMC	ANCHOR	MADEIRA
		Cross stitch in 2 strands		
	•	153	103	0710
	⊞	341	117	0901
	★	444	291	0105
	∴	452	232	1807
	▶	676	891	2208
	▬	720	326	0309
	↑	741	314	0201
	T	798	137	0911
	✕	801	359	2007
	❙	918	341	0314
		3031	1088	2003
		3750	1036	1007
	—	3823	386	0111
	◉	3836	90	0801
		Back stitch in 1 strand		
	——	3031	1088	2003
	▽	Cream beads		
	⊖	Orange beads		

Flutterflies

The pale, wispy shapes of butterflies are set against a background of warm, rich colours. A beaded edging has been added, which matches the colours used in the design, so that it appears as if the beads are extending the size of the mini cushion. Back stitch has been used to outline the butterflies and to give them definition against the lilac background. When adding back stitched outlines it is usually best to avoid using black thread as this can often appear very harsh. A lighter tone such as grey or brown can still define the details of a design but will result in a softer finish.

The rich colours are also ideal for a Christmas design – replace the butterflies with small festive motifs for a lovely mini cushion to place under your tree.

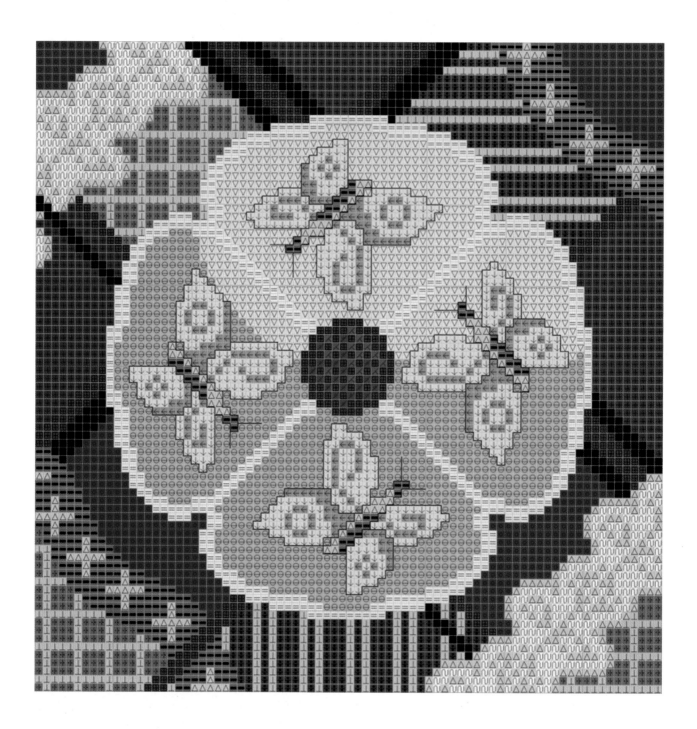

Flutterflies

		DMC	ANCHOR	MADEIRA
		Cross stitch in 2 strands		
	⊖	155	1030	0903
	▽	211	342	0801
	▬	317	400	1714
	✚	327	98	0713
	⊙	347	1025	0407
	↓	369	1043	1309
	△	415	398	1802
	=	746	275	0101
	⊥	772	259	1604
	⊞	829	277	2113
	⊡	895	246	1404
	⊹	3012	844	1613
	■	3021	905	2003
	←	3052	859	1509
	∩	3865	926	White
		Back stitch in 1 strand		
	──	3021	905	2003
	✗	Dark red beads		
	✗	Red beads		

Fossil Frenzy

The shapes and contours of ancient ammonite fossils have been given a modern touch in this mini cushion, with their swirling patterns forming the integral design feature. Natural and man-made grooves carved into the sea-soaked rocks, and fossilized animal tracks are represented by the patterns within the corners of the design, with shades of blue forming a backdrop of sea and sky. The pink cross stitches dotted around the mini cushion achieve a very lively effect and they could be replaced with sparkling pink seed beads for added texture. To create a shimmering sea effect in the areas containing solid blue cross stitches try replacing one strand of blue cotton in your needle with one strand of shiny silver metallic thread.

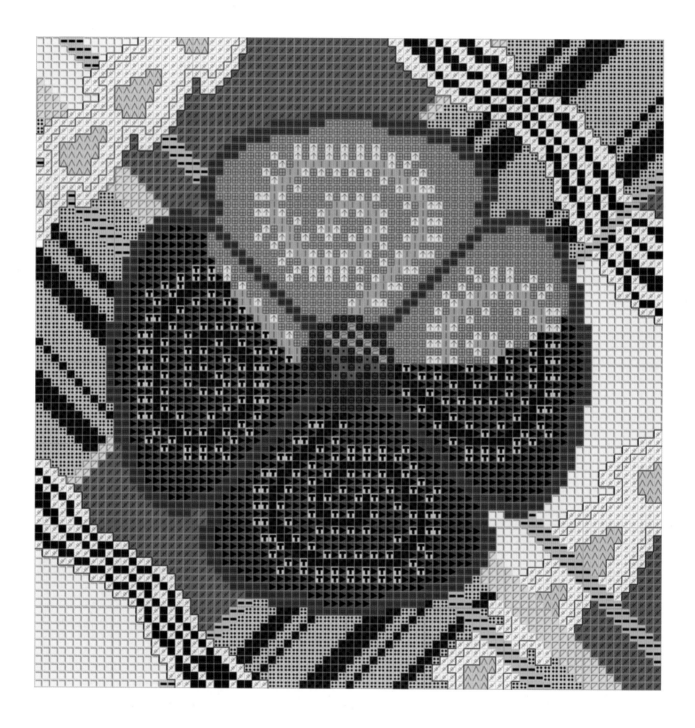

Fossil Frenzy

	DMC	ANCHOR	MADEIRA
Cross stitch in 2 strands			
156+3753	939+1031	0906+1001
300	352	2304
321	47	0510
356	1013	0402
415	398	1802
704	256	1308
727	293	0110
758	868	0403
761	1021	0502
798	137	0911
819	271	0814
828	158	1101
844	1041	1810
930	1035	1712
932	343	1710
938	380	2005
973	290	0105
3818	923	1303
3865	926	White
Back stitch in 1 strand			
844	1041	1810

Swirling Shells

*H*ear the sound of the waves lapping the shore and washing shells across the sandy beach as you stitch these swirling patterns, which represent the shapes of pearlescent periwinkles. Solid areas of light and dark coral shades give a very smooth appearance to the design and the shades of blue add a calming effect to the piece.

Driftwood appears in the corners of the design with links from sea-worn chains caught amongst them. This is a lovely design to stitch in the sun, with clear blue water lapping at your feet. Try replacing the yellow and cream cross stitches that represent the chain links in opposite corners with sparkly gold seed beads to add an extra dimension to the cushion.

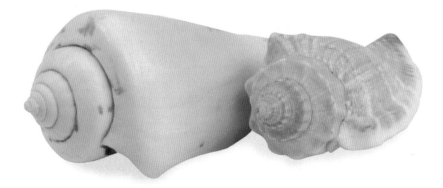

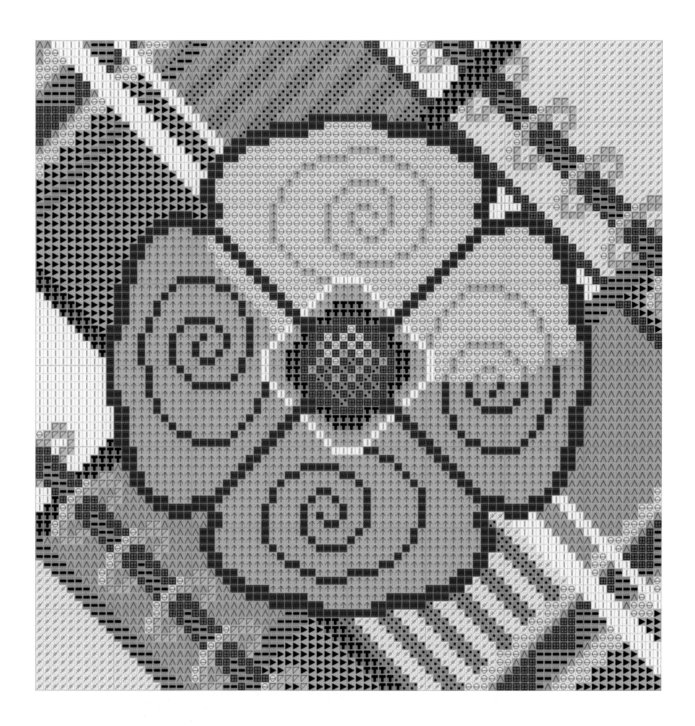

Swirling Shells

		DMC	ANCHOR	MADEIRA
		Cross stitch in 2 strands		
	T	322	978	1004
		355	1014	0401
		422	373	2102
		611	898	2107
	▶	742	303	0107
	◹	744	301	0110
	↑	758	868	0403
	∧	932	343	1710
	✕	3752	1032	1002
	⊖	3770	1009	0306
	◆	3778	1013	2310
			Ecru	926	Ecru

Tropical Forest

Hot, sultry colours of tropical plants and palm trees have been used in this design, where lush green shades and vibrant coral reds help to create the warm, intense atmosphere of being inside a tropical forest, surrounded by earthy colours and exquisite flashes of yellow and orange. The forest theme is continued in several of the patterned blocks where brown animal tracks appear around the design. Two corners feature hints of cool forest streams. The other two corners are adorned with a tribal-influenced pattern of green circles on a black base. Beads have been added around the edge of the mini cushion but seed beads could also be used within the design in place of some of the stranded cotton colours.

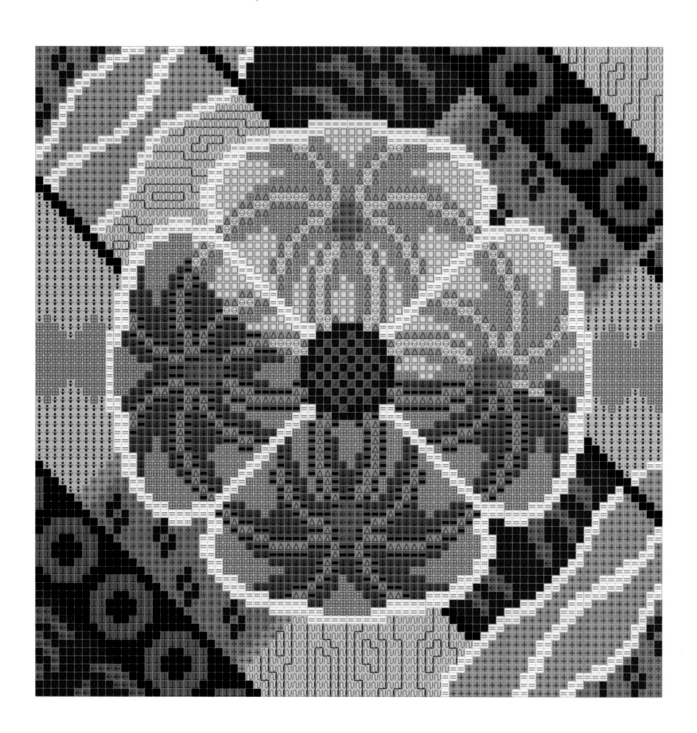

Tropical Forest

Tropical Forest

		DMC	ANCHOR	MADEIRA
		Cross stitch in 2 strands		
	⊖	225	271	0501
	■	310	Black	Black
	▬	349	13	0212
	△	351	10	0214
	□	369	1043	1309
	┼	414	235	1801
	⊞	704	256	1308
	❖	728	305	0113
	▼	801	359	2007
	←	840	1084	1912
	∩∪	842	1080	1910
	↓	904	258	1413
	⊥	905	257	1412
	·⫶·	3853	1003	0307
	=	Blanc	2	White
		Back stitch in 1 strand		
	——	801	359	2007
	⊠	Emerald green beads		

Rusty Leaves

ich red cross stitches outline the autumnal leaves
featured in this design, laying on a bed of olive green.
A variety of patchwork-style patterns appear around the
edges and seed beads that match the two shades of blue in
one of these patterns have been attached to the centre of
the mini cushion.

Cross stitches using the tweeding technique have been
worked into each corner of the cushion and this effect has
been carried through into the beaded edging by alternating
red and yellow beads in each strand. This colour combination
produces a vibrant fiery effect to match the flaming leaves.

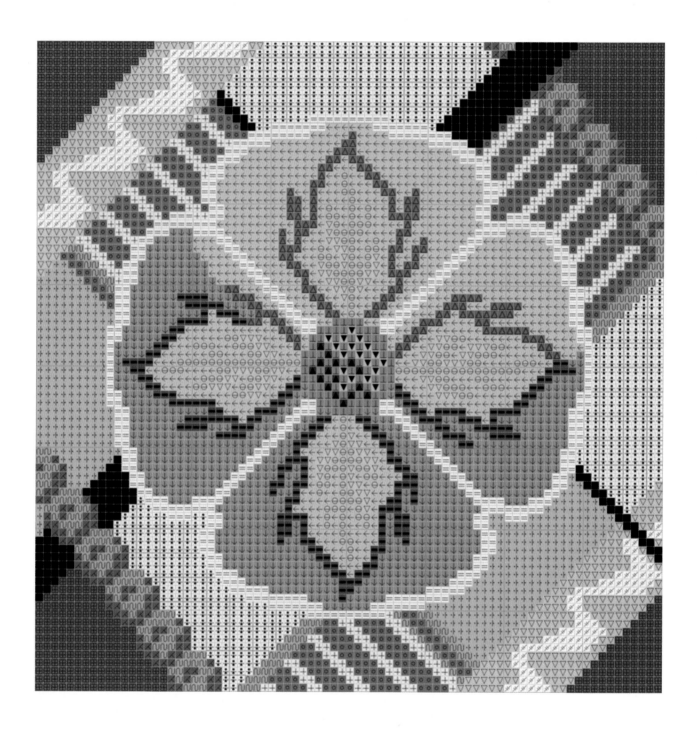

Rusty Leaves

		DMC	ANCHOR	MADEIRA
		Cross stitch in 2 strands		
	■	310	Black	Black
	△	606	335	0209
	·‖·	722	323	0307
	=	762	234	1804
	▽	772	1043	1604
	▬	817	46	0211
	✕	840	1084	1912
	○	931	1034	1711
	⊞	973+606	290+335	0105+0209
	⊖	973	290	0105
	↓	3012	844	1613
	←	3013	854	1605
	⊥	3045	888	2103
	+	3752	1032	1002
	∾	3820	306	2209
	✗	3865	2	White
	÷	Ecru	926	Ecru
		Back stitch in 1 strand		
	——	3045	888	2103
	▲	Dark blue beads		
	▼	Light blue beads		

The Seasons and Special Occasions

Flowers in Spring

Summer Blooms

Summer Blooms Card
and Scissors Keeper

Autumn Leaves

Winter Breeze

Wedding Bouquet

Anniversary Roses

Party Bloom

Christmas Collection

Christmas Cards and Decorations

Flowers in Spring

Delicate flowers begin to appear in the early stages of spring and four such flowers feature in this design. Some deep colours left over from winter can also be seen around the edges of the design, such as moss green, rusty brown and golden yellow, but the pale blue cross stitches burst through these deeper colours, protecting the young flowers from the harsh winter.

Tweeding has been used to great effect, adding soft texture as the blue, pink and lilac shades spread across the mini cushion. Beads have also been attached to the centre of the design and these should always be added after all the cross stitching has been completed.

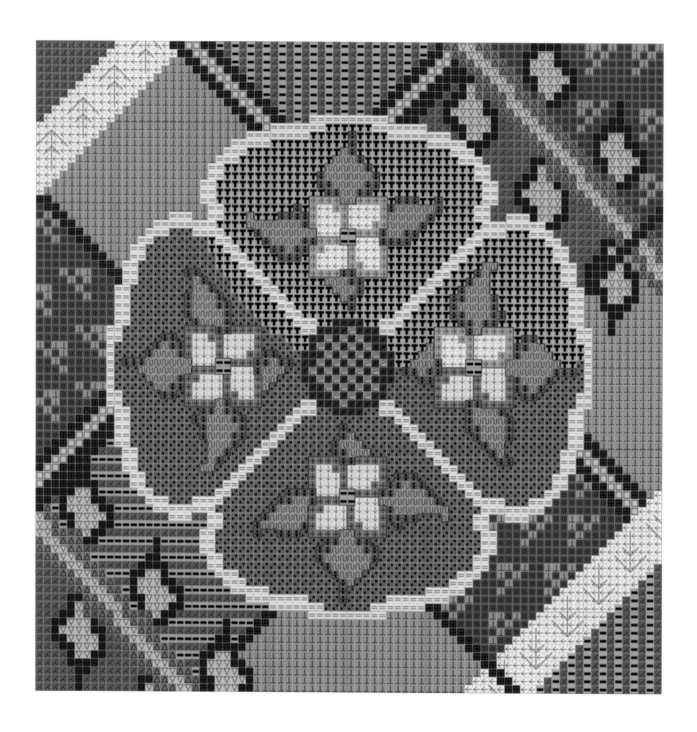

Flowers in Spring

		DMC	ANCHOR	MADEIRA
		Cross stitch in 2 strands		
	T	334+3608	977+86	1003+0709
	⊞	413	400	1713
	☐	415	398	1802
	▬	742	303	0107
	↓	745	301	0111
	=	800	159	1002
	✕	801	359	2007
	△	892	35	0412
	○	920	1004	0312
	∿	993	1070	1201
	✕	3011	924	1607
	▽	3354	74	0606
	+	3607	87	0708
	◆	3607+334	87+977	0708+1003
	·‖·	3608	86	0709
	⊖	3777	1015	0407
	÷	3812	189	1203
	⊥	3824	8	0304
	←	Ecru	926	Ecru
		Back stitch in 1 strand		
	——	413	400	1713
	——	892	35	0412
	⊇	Grey beads		

Summer Blooms

This design is full of the vibrant and succulent colours of summer with four large blooms bursting through. Beads feature quite heavily on this mini cushion within the centre of each flower and in the centre of the whole design. Two colours of beads have been used, creating a chequered effect that is continued in the patterned border, but you could reverse the beaded areas by stitching the flower centres with stranded cotton and adding beads in place of the cross-stitched petals in each bloom.

For a slightly more subtle design, cross stitch each of the blooms using shades of pink thread and leave the surrounding area within the ginger border unstitched, allowing the white fabric to show through.

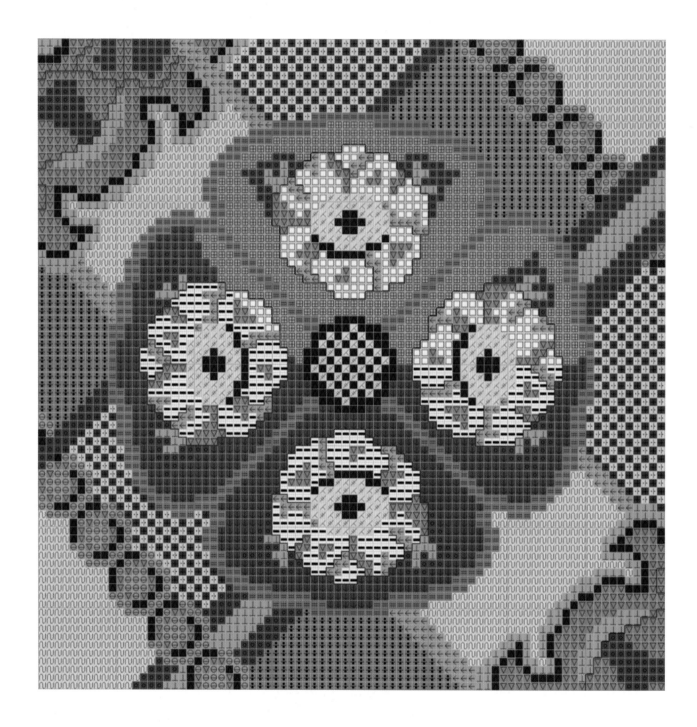

Summer Blooms

*Colour variation for
Summer Blooms*

Summer Blooms

		DMC	ANCHOR	MADEIRA
		Cross stitch in 2 strands		
	·ǀ·	211	342	0801
	↓	304	1006	0511
	∩∪	369	1043	1309
	←	414	235	1801
	▽	435	1046	2010
	⊥	704	256	1308
	▲	801	359	2007
	÷	826	977	1012
	⊞	899	66	0609
	○	3818	923	1303
	=	3826	1049	2306
	+	3837	99	0712
	⊖	3864	376	2309
	☐	5200	1	White
	▬	Ecru	926	Ecru
		Back stitch in 1 strand		
	——	801	359	2007
	⤬	Powder blue beads		
	⋏	Powder pink beads		

Summer Blooms Card and Scissors Keeper

x x x x x x x x x x x x x x x x x x x x

One of the bloom motifs has been used in this matching card. You could try replacing the purple cross stitches with the vibrant blue or pale green shades used on the mini cushion.

This design can also be made into a scissors keeper. Stitch the circular part of the design, up to and including the ginger border and make into a round cushion following the mini cushion make-up instructions. Sandwich a loop of narrow ribbon which is one-and-a-half times the width of the design, between the stitching and the backing fabric. Then pass the loop of ribbon through one handle of the scissors and push the small cushion through the ribbon loop.

See 'Making up a Greetings Card' on page 170

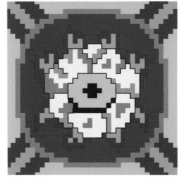 

Colour variations for the Summer Blooms Card and Scissors Keeper

Summer Blooms Card and Scissors Keeper

		DMC	ANCHOR	MADEIRA
		Cross stitch in 2 strands		
	·|·	211	342	0801
	↓	304	1006	0511
	←	414	235	1801
	▽	435	1046	2010
	⊥	704	256	1308
	▲	801	359	2007
	○	3818	923	1303
	+	3837	99	0712
	☐	5200	1	White
		Back stitch in 1 strand		
	——	801	359	2007

Autumn Leaves

Many rich colours are seen in the autumn when leaves and foliage change from lush fresh greens to warm browns, burnt oranges and golden yellows. These glorious colours have been gathered together in this autumnal design. The blue shades of a changing autumn sky also appear and the central feature of crisp brown leaves incorporate tweeding to produce mixed, textured shades of earthy brown. Hints of green foliage can also be seen peeping through the carpet of fallen leaves in the centre of the design. As there are only a few yellow stitches in the design, it would be quick and easy to replace them with yellow seed beads to add extra interest.

Autumn Leaves

		DMC	ANCHOR	MADEIRA
		Cross stitch in 2 strands		
	▽	371	854	2110
	A	414	235	1801
	B	415	398	1802
	⊞	702	226	1306
	★	722+371	323+854	0307+2110
	⊖	722	323	0307
	●	815	44	0513
	⧅	907	255	1410
	⚡	973	290	0105
	◣	975	370	2303
	▼	975+3778	370+1013	2303+2310
	✳	986	246	1313
	■	3021	905	2003
	▪▪	3033	390	2001
	C	3072	847	1805
	⦂	3760	1039	1106
	=	3778	1013	2310
	♥	3815	877	1205
	⑂	3817	875	1209
	+	3840	120	0907

Winter Breeze

Imagine a windy winter's day with crisp and crunchy leaves whipping through the air. Such natural energy has been captured in this design with icy shades of turquoise in the swirling leaves and warmer tones of brown and orange to reflect the sun casting its early evening shadows. The small hints of pink and deep red have been included to add a touch of sweetness to an otherwise sharp design.

The texture of bare trees and rough bark has been created by using the tweeding technique in which two very different shades of thread have been combined into the one needle.

Winter Breeze

		DMC	ANCHOR	MADEIRA
		Cross stitch in 2 strands		
	⊞	309	39	0507
	▽	407	914	2312
	+	444	291	0105
	□	605	60	0613
	÷	677	886	2207
	◼	814	45	0514
	∩	822	926	1908
	▬	869	375	2105
	=	907	255	1410
	╱	922+869	1003+375	0311+2105
	⋮	922	1003	0311
	↓	958	187	1114
	⊖	993	1070	1201
	⊡	3743	869	0807
	⫽	3746	1030	0903
	△	3819	279	1414
	○	3819+922	279+1003	1414+0311
	←	3830	5975	0401
	✗	3865	926	White

x x x x x x x x x x x x x x x x x x x x x x x x x

Wedding Bouquet

Delicate rosebuds form a small bouquet surrounded by tiny cross-stitched dots of confetti floating in the air within this design. Although pink and green have been chosen as the main colour theme, it is easy to adapt the colours in this design to suit those chosen for a particular wedding. Try stitching lilac rosebuds surrounded by cream or gold threads, or choose gorgeous red rosebuds for a very romantic design.

The rosebud motifs could also be stitched and mounted on their own as thank you cards or to make lovely additions to the covers of wedding invitations. A tassel and loop were added at the making-up stage so that the finished piece could be hung on a wall, banister or door handle as a wedding decoration. It is lovely to keep as a lasting memento of that special day.

x x x x x x x x x x x x x x x x x x x x x x x x x

Colour variations for Wedding Bouquet

Wedding Bouquet

		DMC	ANCHOR	MADEIRA
		Cross stitch in 2 strands		
	✕	318	399	1802
	▽	372	853	2110
	■	535	1041	1809
	◆◆	603	55	0701
	⊖	644	830	2001
	✳	699	230	1303
	⊞	783	307	2211
	◆•	819	271	0814
	↑	3347	265	1503
	=	3716	25	0606
		Back stitch in 1 strand		
	——	535	1041	1809

x x x x x x x x x x x x x x x x x x x x x x x x x x x x x x x

Anniversary Roses

To commemorate that special anniversary, this versatile design can be adapted to all. Ruby, coral or sapphire anniversaries, for example, can all be celebrated by changing the colour of the white roses to match. There is also a touch of lace within the design from the pale grey and white corner motifs and seed beads have been added for extra sparkle.

The dark and light blue pattern is ideal for personalizing with your own choice of colour scheme.

For that someone special, stitch one of the roses on its own in shades of red for a romantic Valentine's card.

x x x x x x x x x x x x x x x x x x x x x x x x x x x x x x x

Colour variations for Anniversary Roses

Anniversary Roses

		DMC	ANCHOR	MADEIRA
		Cross stitch in 2 strands		
	■	317	400	1714
	↑	318	399	1802
	◩	347	1025	0407
	▶	368	214	1310
	•	422	373	2102
	⬛•	561	217	1205
	═	680	901	2210
	✕	825	162	1011
	⊖	905	257	1412
	⊞	3047	852	2205
	∧	3840	120	0907
	—	Blanc	2	White
		Back stitch in 1 strand		
	—	3799	236	1708
	⅂	Grey beads		

Party Bloom

This vivid design would make an ideal gift for celebrating a special occasion with its bold patterns, balloon-like shapes and mouth-watering colours.

Shades of grey can make a design appear rather dull, but surround them with citrus orange and yellow and sorbet pinks as in this design and they are instantly lifted.

To add sparkle to this design, replace one strand of grey thread with one strand of glittering silver thread and your cross stitches will shine. Further embellishments could be made by adding a beaded edging around the mini cushion. Follow the instructions on page 168, using brightly coloured beads to finish this sumptuous project.

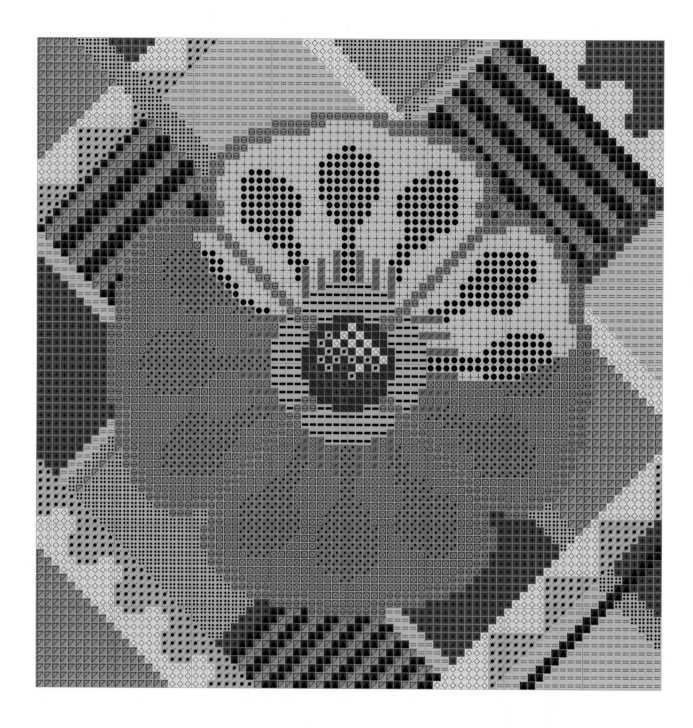

Party Bloom

		DMC	ANCHOR	MADEIRA
		Cross stitch in 2 strands		
	◆	322	978	1004
	◕	352	9	0303
	◫	402	1047	2307
	⊠	415	398	1802
	◹	740	316	0202
	=	743	305	0113
	◇	754	1012	0305
	✕	782+989	308+240	2212+1401
	●	809	175	0909
	▲	815	44	0513
	◣	869	375	2105
	▬	958	187	1114
	⊖	989	240	1401
	+	3072	847	1805
	✳	3804	62	0703

Christmas Collection

𝒜 festive home is not complete without a gorgeous red poinsettia plant, so what better way to celebrate the holiday season than with a glorious floral design. Wintry motifs of holly, berries and branches of fir trees decorate the corners of the Poinsettia cushion, with white and green tweeding giving the effect of frosted grass. Snowflakes are dotted around the edge of the design using a cool shade of grey thread. But the main feature of this design is the poinsettia flower, which appears in three shades of red stranded cotton.

The Joyful Christmas cushion features bells, mistletoe, holly and roses, surrounded by a rich tartan pattern in warm colours. There are plenty of opportunities for adding seed beads to this design, such as replacing the red holly berry stitches, or the single stitches that are dotted around the Christmas roses.

Joyful Christmas Cushion

		DMC	ANCHOR	MADEIRA
		Cross stitch in 2 strands		
		301	1049	2306
		321	47	0510
	★	415	398	1802
		444	291	0105
	▽	676	891	2208
	♥	783	307	2211
	•	794	121	0907
	■	801	359	2007
		904	258	1413
	⊖	907	255	1410
	✳	3708	31	0408
	■	3750	1036	1007
		3823	386	0111
		Blanc	2	White
		Back stitch in 1 strand		
	——	310	Black	Black

Poinsettia Cushion

		DMC	ANCHOR	MADEIRA
		Cross stitch in 2 strands		
	·|·	414	235	1801
	⊥	498	1006	0511
	←	502	876	1703
	▼	699	230	1303
	○	760	1022	0405
	■	801	359	2007
	⊖	814	45	0514
	□	907+Blanc	255+2	1410+White
	∿	907	255	1410
	∔	931	1034	1711
	△	943	188	1203
	▬	959	185	1113
	↓	3051	269	1508
	⊞	3052	859	1509
	=	3829	901	2212
		Back stitch in 1 strand		
	——	814	45	0514

The single poinsettia, holiday bells and Christmas rose motifs have also been used on a set of greetings cards. The poinsettia card incorporates the snowflake design that appears in the cushion, but you could replace these snowflakes with the olive green stripes that feature in the cushion corners for yet another card design to add to your collection.

Christmas Poinsettia Card

		DMC	ANCHOR	MADEIRA
		Cross stitch in 2 strands		
	·ᑊ·	414	235	1801
	⊥	498	1006	0511
	○	760	1022	0405
	■	814	45	0514
	△	943	188	1203
	▬	959	185	1113
	⬇	3051	269	1508
	⊞	3052	859	1509
	═	3829	901	2212
		Back stitch in 1 strand		
	——	814	45	0514

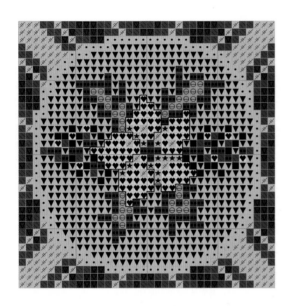

In place of the white stranded cotton within the Christmas rose petals, try cross stitching with two strands of shiny silver metallic thread and add beads in place of the single white and red cross stitches for a card that will really shine. If using metallic threads, always use a shorter length than you would normally use when stitching with stranded cotton to avoid knotting or snagging the fine metal strands.

Joyful Christmas Rose Card

		DMC	ANCHOR	MADEIRA
		Cross stitch in 2 strands		
	◨	321	47	0510
	★	415	398	1802
	✕	444	291	0105
	▼	676	891	2208
	•	794	121	0907
	■	801	359	2007
	▬	904	258	1413
	⊖	907	255	1410
	◤	3750	1036	1007
	♥	Blanc	2	White
		Back stitch in 1 strand		
═	——	310	Black	Black

To make these bells really shimmer, try replacing one of the strands of cotton in your needle with shiny gold metallic thread when stitching the golden bells. You could also leave a ¼in (6mm) border of plain fabric around each edge of the design and then fray the edges for two rows. Fold a piece of gold card in half and attach the stitching to the front of it for a different type of Christmas card.

Joyful Christmas Bells Card

		DMC	ANCHOR	MADEIRA
		Cross stitch in 2 strands		
		301	1049	2306
		321	47	0510
		444	291	0105
		676	891	2208
		794	121	0907
		801	359	2007
		3708	31	0408
		3750	1036	1007
		3823	386	0111
		Back stitch in 1 strand		
		310	Black	Black

A single poinsettia flower from the cushion design has been used to create a gorgeous tree decoration, which heavily incorporates the use of red seed beads. This adds some dimension to the design by lifting the flower out from the green cross-stitched leaves.

In contrast to the square shape of the poinsettia decoration, two diamond-shaped decorations have also been made, this time using the holly and mistletoe motifs from the Joyful Christmas cushion. For an alternative to the square or diamond-shaped decorations, only stitch the part of the design within – and including – the cross-stitched circle, and then make up into a small round cushion to hang on your tree.

Christmas Poinsettia Hanging Tree Decoration

		DMC	ANCHOR	MADEIRA
		Cross stitch in 2 strands		
	←	502	876	1703
	▼	699	230	1303
	△	943	188	1203
	▬	959	185	1113
	◣	3051	269	1508
	⊞	3052	859	1509
	═	3829	901	2212
	▯	Bright red beads		
	○	Dusky pink beads		
	●	Deep red beads		

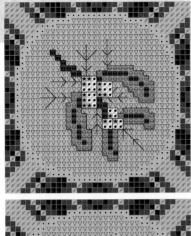

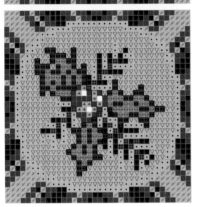

These tree decorations are very simple to make: follow the guidelines for making up a mini cushion once all of the cross stitching and back stitching is complete and any beads have been added. Ensure a loop of ribbon or braid is sandwiched between the stitching and backing fabric before making up the decoration so that it can be hung on the tree. Or, instead of using ribbon or braid, try plaiting one length each of red, blue and yellow stranded cotton to make a matching loop, which carries through the tartan theme as shown here. You may also want to trim the edges of one or two of the cross-stitched items with gold braid or shiny beads for that extra Christmassy finish.

Joyful Christmas Holly and Mistletoe Decorations

		DMC	ANCHOR	MADEIRA
		Cross stitch in 2 strands		
		301	1049	2306
		321	47	0510
		415	398	1802
		444	291	0105
		676	891	2208
		794	121	0907
		904	258	1413
		907	255	1410
		3708	31	0408
		3750	1036	1007
		3865	926	White
		Back stitch in 1 strand		
		310	Black	Black

Contemporary Design and Games

Blue Harmony

Kaleidoscope

Candyfloss

Myth and Magic

Golden Stripes

Taste of India

Joker in the Pack

Checkmate

Blue Harmony

As the name of this mini cushion suggests, various shades of blue, from pale and dusky to dark and electric sit together in harmony within this design. The grey, yellow and golden shades of stranded cotton help to achieve this harmonious effect by acting as barriers between the different hues of blue, defining the individual patterns. The main pattern gives the impression of a heavy brocade fabric.

One of the colours has been created using the 'tweeding' technique, producing a unique shade of blue that cannot be achieved with one stranded cotton colour alone. Try experimenting with this technique: one strand of yellow and one strand of blue threaded in your needle together will provide a very interesting effect.

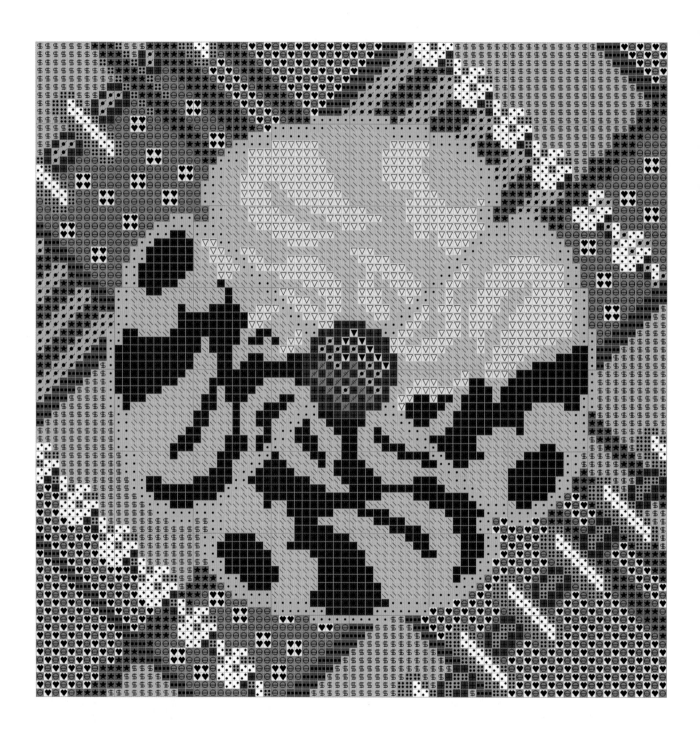

Blue Harmony

		DMC	ANCHOR	MADEIRA
		Cross stitch in 2 strands		
	✳	336	149	1007
	✏	437	362	2012
	★	451	233	1808
	▼	677	886	2207
	♥	775	975	1001
	⚃	783	307	2211
	╲╲	794	121	0907
	▽	794+3072	121+847	0907+1805
	■■	797	147	0912
	✚	869	375	2105
	✕	970	316	0203
	•	973	290	0105
	＄	3072	847	1805
	⊖	3760	1039	1106
	◆•	Blanc	2	White

Kaleidoscope

As a kaleidoscope turns, the colourful images inside constantly change and it is just one of these images that has been captured here. This design is full of sweeping curves with an assortment of bright and buzzing colours and patterns mixed together to draw your eye into the centre of the cushion. The cushion is a joy to stitch, with its wide range of playful colours and interesting patterns.

There are many blocks of solid colour, which makes this design ideal for experimenting with. Try replacing the stranded cotton with beads and metallic threads.

Mini Cushions in Cross Stitch

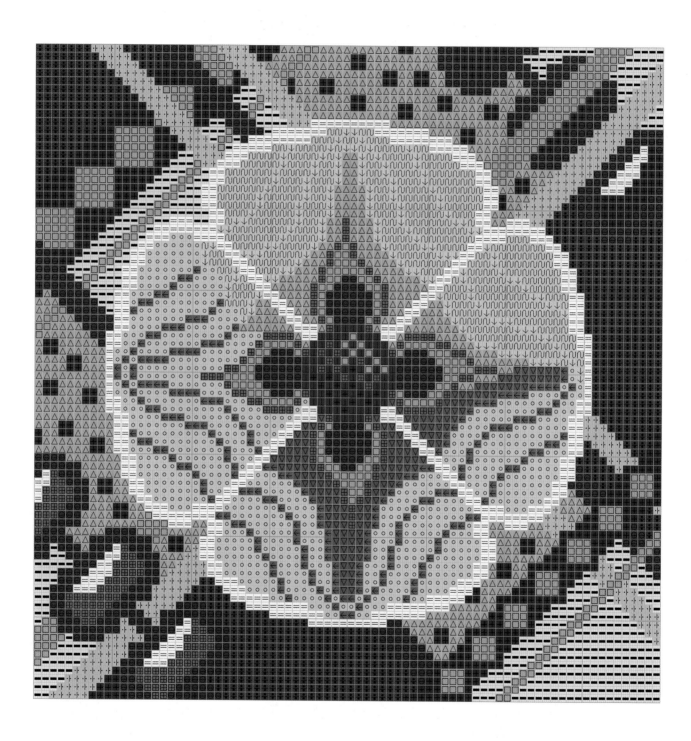

Kaleidoscope

		DMC	ANCHOR	MADEIRA
		Cross stitch in 2 strands		
	▬	225	271	0501
	⊖	327	98	0713
	↓	415	398	1802
	←	451	233	1808
	✛	700	227	1304
	∿	778	1016	0808
	⊥⊥	869	375	2105
	⊞	930	1035	1712
	☐	932	343	1710
	·⫯·	973	290	0105
	○	3354	74	0606
	△	3608	86	0709
	▽	3803	69	0602
	✚	3807	122	0905
	=	3865	926	White

Candyfloss

Sorbet shades and sugar pinks feature heavily in this design, along with pastel blue and lilac and a snappy deep red. This is a young and fun design to brighten up a dressing table. Stiff stripes appear like ribbons criss-crossing the design. In keeping with this theme, try sandwiching strips of ribbon between the stitched fabric and the backing fabric when making up the mini cushion and stitch a loop of ribbon to one corner so that the finished piece can be hung on a wall. Then attach brightly coloured glass beads to the ends of the ribbons.

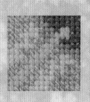

Candyfloss

	DMC	ANCHOR	MADEIRA
	Cross stitch in 2 strands		
=	165	278	1414
□	211	342	0801
▼	327	98	0713
←	340	1030	0902
▬	351	10	0214
△	352	9	0303
✕	602+3609	63+85	0702+0710
⊞	602	63	0702
∩∪	800	159	1002
·⊦·	818	48	0608
▮	902	897	0601
✚	963	73	0607
▼	975	370	2303
+	3609	85	0710
⊙	3726	1018	0810
⊖	3843	410	1102

Myth and Magic

Celtic crosses appear as mysterious motifs in this mini cushion, with magical colours and shapes surrounding them in the patchwork background. Hints of magical shapes influenced by soft feathers and hard crystals appear in the corners of the design, which would not be complete without some dazzling seed beads. Try attaching some gold charms or shiny buttons onto the pale green areas of the stitching to add your own magical touch to the design.

The beaded edging adds to the vibrancy of the finished mini cushion but in place of some of the beaded strands, try threading on some gorgeous pearls or larger crystal droplets randomly around the edge for an even more magical effect.

Myth and Magic

		DMC	ANCHOR	MADEIRA
		Cross stitch in 2 strands		
	△	414	235	1801
	■	415	398	1802
	⊞	602	63	0702
	□	772	259	1604
	■	839	1050	1913
	←	920	1004	0312
	↓	3012	844	1613
	⊥	3041	871	0806
	=	3326	36	0606
	○	3743	869	0807
	■	3799	236	1713
	+	3820	306	2209
	■	3857	896	0811
	·│·	Ecru	926	Ecru
		Back stitch in 1 strand		
	——	3799	236	1713
	✕	Gold beads		
	∩∪	Pale grey beads		

Golden Stripes

This design has captured the spirit of the African jungle, with its animal prints and dusky, earthy colours. The golden stripes represent the sun's hot rays exuding from an intense red heat that sears across the smooth grey rocks.

To create a larger picture for framing, stitch the mini cushion design onto a larger piece of fabric and cross stitch a 1in (25mm) border around each edge of the design, which incorporates the white, brown and orange motif.

A larger cushion could also be created by stitching four versions of this design on one large piece of fabric, but in two of those versions replace the threads used to stitch the golden stripes with shades that reflect different times of the day. Use dusky blues and lilacs for the break of dawn and deep fiery reds for the sunset.

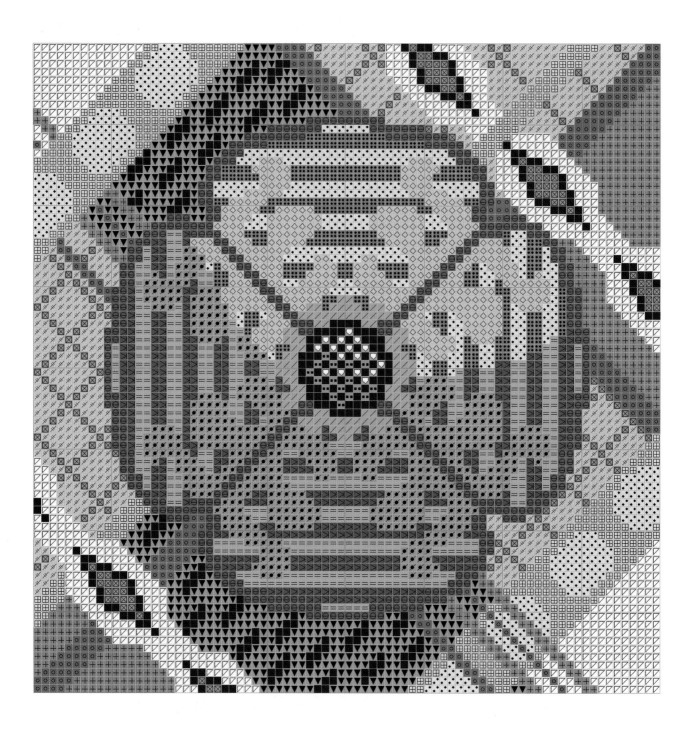

Design variation for Golden Stripes

Golden Stripes

		DMC	ANCHOR	MADEIRA
		Cross stitch in 2 strands		
	▷	434	310	2009
	▓	435	1046	2010
	╱	451	233	1808
	✎	453	231	1806
	⊞	605	60	0613
	▼	734	280	1610
	⊠	741	314	0201
	=	742	303	0107
	∴	745	301	0111
	◇	762	234	1804
	○	926	850	1707
	■	938	380	2005
	+	961	38	0506
	⊖	3801	29	0411
	✕	3855	311	2301
	◹	5200	1	White
	▪▪	Lime green beads		
	▽	Orange beads		

Taste of India

The dusty, hazy colours of India's landscape appear in this mini cushion design, which incorporates interpretations of the patterns found in intricate jewellery and henna tattoos worn by the women of India. For a slight twist, there is an even smaller cushion, which has been attached to one corner of the larger cushion with a beautiful tassel to finish it off (its corresponding chart is on page 145). It also features a loop of braid so that the finished project can be hung on a wall.

Before making up the two cushions, remember to sandwich the braid and tassel in the correct place between the stitching and the backing fabric (see page 167).

Chart for large Taste of India cushion

Chart for small cushion attachment

Taste of India

	DMC	ANCHOR	MADEIRA
	Cross stitch in 2 strands		
⊠	300	352	2304
▽	300+612	352+853	2304+2108
◉	310	Black	Black
÷	341	117	0901
⊖	415	398	1802
⋅⫶	612	853	2108
←	738+950	942+376	2013+2309
⊞	738	942	2013
↓	738+436	942+1045	2013+2011
◣	792	941	0905
∿	813	161	1013
+	922	1003	0311
=	973	290	0105
□	3012	844	1613
⊥	3363	262	1602

Joker in the Pack

$\mathscr{B}$old patterns in primary colours fill the pictures in a deck of playing cards. These patterns have been re-worked and combined in this mini cushion, which would make an ideal gift for a gaming friend or relative.

The Jack, Queen, King and the cheeky face of the Joker feature in this design and any one of these could be stitched alone to create a matching greetings card, or mounted on the top of a box in which to keep a deck of cards.

Create a larger cushion by stitching combinations of the heart, diamond, clubs and spades, along with the different patterns used within the cushion design in rows and columns.

Use a piece of graph paper to help plot the stitches.

Large cushion design for Joker in the Pack

Joker in the Pack

		DMC	ANCHOR	MADEIRA
		Cross stitch in 2 strands		
■	▲	310	Black	Black
▨	♡	444	291	0105
▨	◆	505	210	1213
▨	○	754	1012	0305
▨	▽	797	147	0912
▨	✚	817	46	0211
		Back stitch in 1 strand		
═	——	797	147	0912

Checkmate

Only six shades of stranded cotton have been used to stitch this design for an avid chess fan, featuring the king, queen, knight, rook and pawn. Much of the Aida fabric is left unstitched, which makes the design quick to complete. For an alternative design, try reversing the black and white effect by cross stitching the white areas with black stranded cotton and leaving the black areas as unstitched fabric.

To create a larger cushion, stitch four versions of the design on one large piece of fabric, either keeping to the colours as they appear in the design or by reversing the black and white pattern, described above. Alternatively, try surrounding the design with blocks of black and white to form a chessboard pattern. The finished piece could also be framed as a picture.

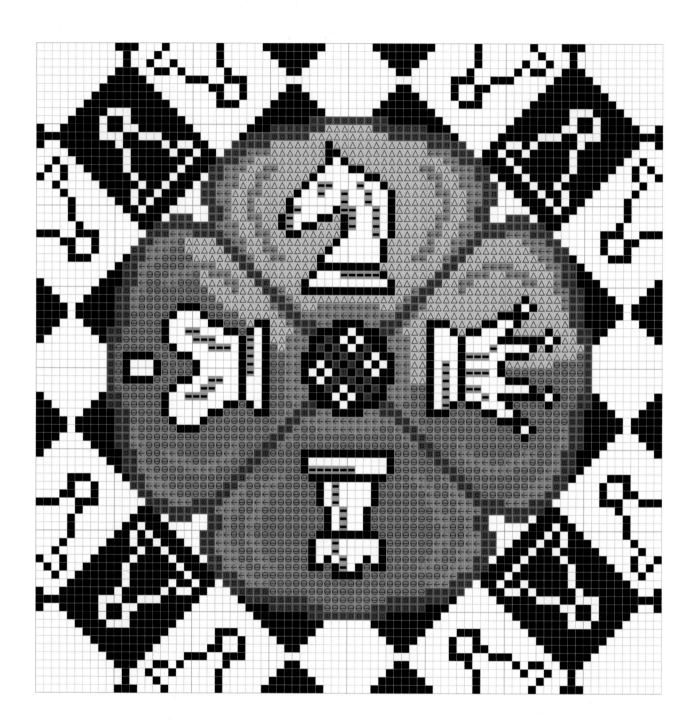

Design variations for Checkmate

Checkmate

		DMC	ANCHOR	MADEIRA
		Cross stitch in 2 strands		
	■	310	Black	Black
	▬	318	399	1802
	←	3765	169	1108
	⊡	3777	1015	0407
	△	3782	831	1906
	⊖	3863	378	1911

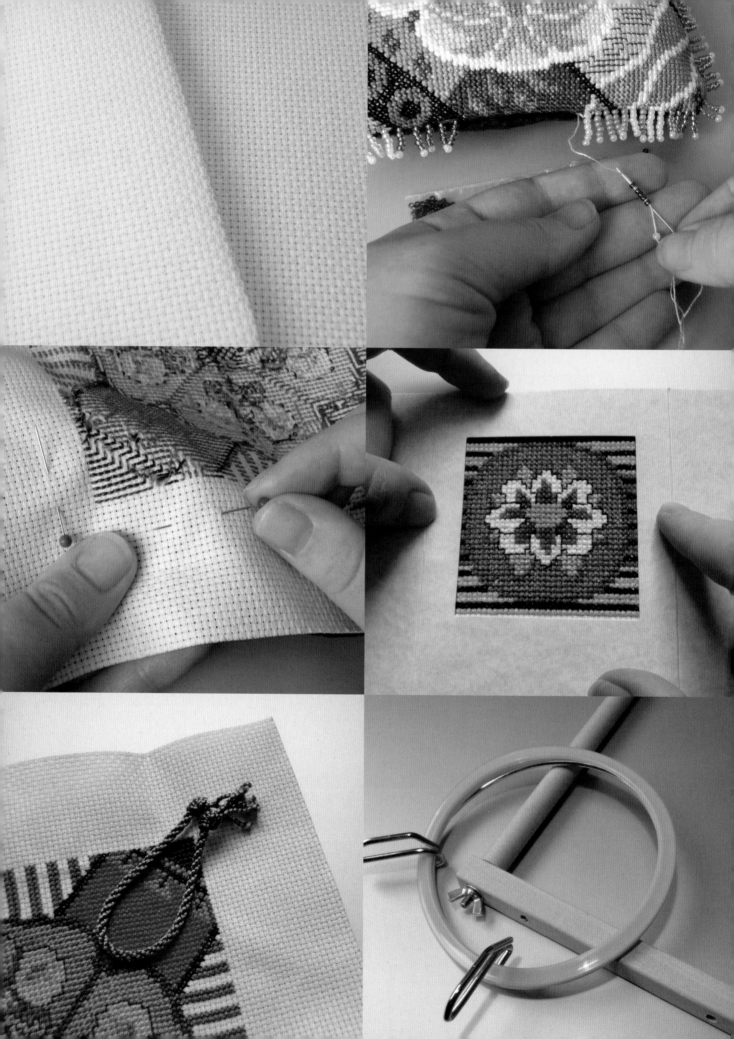

Materials and Stitching Know-how

Materials Required

Before you can begin a stitching project you will need to gather some materials. You may already have some of these materials in your sewing basket but if not, they are all readily available from your local needlecraft or sewing store and can increasingly be obtained via mail order companies and the internet.

Fabrics

Fabrics for cross stitch are available in a multitude of colours and should either be an evenweave or a blockweave fabric so as to produce evenly stitched crosses. Evenweave fabrics, such as linen and quaker cloth, require very careful counting when stitching as they are closely woven with the same number of threads up and across the fabric (known as the warp and weft), resulting in a very fine grid on which to work. Blockweave fabric, in particular Aida, is the most widely used fabric for cross stitch as the woven threads form small blocks which can be easily counted – ideal for transferring counted cross stitch designs from chart to fabric. Both evenweave and blockweave fabrics are measured by their count of holes per inch, or HPI, with the most commonly used counts being 28HPI for evenweave and 14HPI for blockweave. Stitching on 28HPI evenweave fabric is equal to stitching on 14HPI blockweave because you would stitch over two threads on evenweave but only over one block on blockweave. Therefore a row of 14 stitches equals 1in (25mm). One point to remember is that the lower the number of holes per inch, the larger the stitches will be, therefore affecting the finished size of your work.

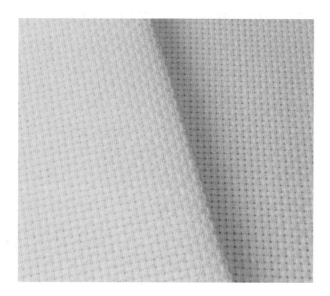

Threads

The threads most commonly used for cross stitching are stranded embroidery cottons – also known as floss – although other threads such as metallics can be used to create different textures on the fabric. Each stranded cotton is sold in either a 26ft 6in or 33ft (8m or 10m) length, which is loosely twisted upon itself to form a small bundle called a skein. Each skein is labelled with its own shade number and is made up of six strands lightly twisted together. Before stitching any project, these strands must be separated and re-combined to ensure the stitching lies flat without the thread being twisted.

For cross stitching, two strands of thread should be re-combined and used to stitch on 14HPI Aida (or 28HPI evenweave), giving an even coverage of the fabric. Using just one strand will create a subtle effect, allowing the fabric to show through, whereas using three strands will give a deeper, solid effect by completely covering the fabric. Detail and outlining have been added to some of the designs in this book by using back stitch with only one strand in a dark shade of thread. Use lengths of stranded cotton that are no longer than 18in (457mm) to help avoid knots (metallic threads should be less than half this length). Should the thread become slightly twisted when stitching, let the needle hang down from the back of your work and allow the thread to unwind.

Stranded embroidery cottons are available in hundreds of shades and for each project in this book you will find a key giving details of coloured cottons. The DMC brand of threads were used to stitch these projects but shade numbers have also been provided for the Anchor and Madeira brands. However, although the shades have been matched across the brands as closely as possible, they will not be exact matches with the DMC brand and this may slightly affect the finished design. It is advisable not to mix threads from differing brands within the one project.

On the mini cushions a number of patterns have been incorporated into each design and you could substitute some of the recommended colours with remnants of thread from other projects or use any leftovers that you may have in your stitching basket. You will see on each cushion that the top right third of each large flower has been stitched with slightly lighter shades of thread to the rest of the design. This is to give the impression of a light source shining on the flower, saturating the colour from it, but again, there are no limits to experimenting with the colours in the designs by changing the shades of thread used.

Beads

There are many kinds of beads that can be used for embroidery but 'seed beads' are the best kind to use when following a chart. Seed beads are small, round glass beads available in a wide range of colours and finishes including opaque, transparent and metallic.

When attached to 14HPI Aida or 28HPI evenweave, seed beads will each cover one small block on the fabric and sit evenly next to each other without pulling or puckering the fabric. This means that cross stitches can be replaced with beads to add a textured embellishment. In this book, the keys beside each of the designs contain only the name of the bead colour to allow for any brand of beads to be used.

Needles

For cross stitching on 14HPI Aida, either a size 24 or 26 blunt-ended tapestry needle should be used. For adding back stitched outlining and detail to a design, a size 26 needle is preferable as it will pierce through holes in the fabric that may already be packed with cross stitches. A size 26 needle is also recommended when stitching on evenweave fabrics

as a bigger size needle can enlarge the holes in the weave of the fabric and affect the finished look of your stitching. An added luxury are gold-plated needles, which are longer lasting than some nickel-plated needles and slip through the fabric with ease, making them a joy to stitch with.

For adding beads to your work, it is necessary to use beading needles, which are thin enough to pass through the holes in the seed beads. Or you could use quilting needles, which are shorter, but are still thin enough to pass through the beads.

Hoops and frames

Some stitchers like to hold their work in their hands while stitching, but others prefer to keep their fabric taut by using an embroidery hoop or frame and there are various kinds available. However, as the designs in this book are relatively small you may find it easier to hold the fabric in your hands.

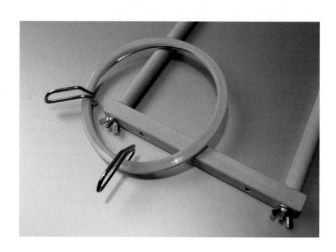

Scissors

A good pair of sharp scissors is a must for all forms of embroidery, as threads need to be cleanly cut without being pulled. It is a good idea to have one pair of scissors just for cutting fabric and a smaller pair solely for snipping thread.

Storage

It is a good idea to keep all your threads, needles and scissors to hand so that you can enjoy sitting down to stitch without interruption. Threads should be kept in a place where they are not squashed, or this will have a detrimental effect on your stitching by allowing specks of fabric to show through the stitches or giving an uneven finish to your work. Fabric should be kept covered up when not in use, such as in a clean pillowcase or rolled inside a tube (such as a kitchen roll tube) which will avoid creases. It is not a good idea to store sewing materials such as fabric and threads in plastic bags as these can attract dust, which will transfer to your materials when you remove them from the bag. Scissors and needles should always be stored somewhere safe, such as a tin or sewing box, and never be tempted to leave your needle in your fabric when not stitching for a period of time as you may find the needle has tarnished and left a stain on your fabric when you return to it.

Materials required for the projects

Mini cushions

- 14HPI Aida fabric 9 x 9in (23 x 23cm).
- Backing fabric 9 x 9in (23 x 23cm). This should preferably be a soft velvet but any material can be used.
- One skein of each cotton colour listed in the key.
- Size 26 tapestry needle.
- Soft toy/cushion filling.
- Strong sewing thread (white) for stitching the cross-stitched fabric and backing fabric together.
- Sewing pins.

Additional materials

- Seed or rocailles beads
- Beading/quilting needle
- Tassel/braid, if hanging the finished piece on a wall
- 14HPI Aida fabric 4 x 4in (10 x 10cm)
- Two-fold card with 2¾in (67mm) square aperture
- Double-sided sticky tape

Now that you have all your materials, the next step is to learn the basic techniques for starting a thread, making cross stitches and back stitches and finishing off your thread. Some designs require other techniques and you will find out how to work them in the instructions that accompany those designs.

Stitching Know-how

Before stitching

Before starting any stitching project, you need to make sure that your chosen fabric is large enough to take the whole design with several inches of spare fabric all around the edge. If you are framing your picture, you should allow at least 2in (50mm) of spare fabric around the edges of the design, but for the mini cushions you should only need to allow 1½in (38mm).

With any project, you should centre the design onto your fabric to ensure that you will be able to fit in the whole design. To do this, fold the fabric in half lengthways and make a light crease, open it up and fold in half again widthways to make another light crease. The point at which the creases cross is the centre of your fabric and the place where you should start your stitching, working from the centre of the chart.

Starting a thread

To begin stitching, pass the threaded needle through the fabric from wrong side to right and leave about 1in (25mm) of thread on the wrong side. As you stitch, hold this loose thread against the fabric and secure it under each stitch. If you prefer, you could leave the loose thread at the back of your work and then darn it under your stitches when you have finished (**1a**).

Cross stitch

Each colour cotton to be used in a design will have a corresponding square on the chart containing a symbol.

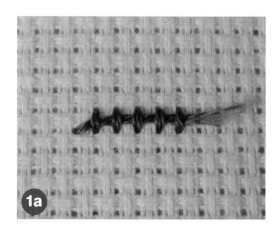

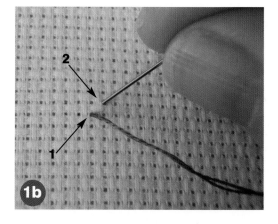

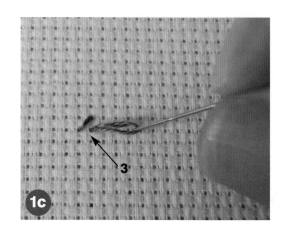

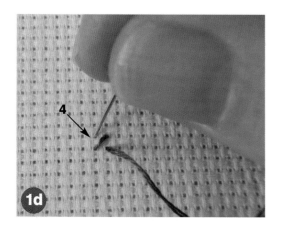

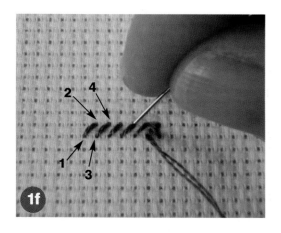

One square on the chart represents one cross stitch or one bead on the fabric.

A cross stitch is made up of two half stitches that cross each other diagonally. Referring to the photographs, push the needle up at 1 and down at 2 to make a half stitch (**1b**), then push the needle up at 3 (**1c**) and down at 4, making another half stitch (**1d**) to complete one cross stitch (**1e**).

If there are blocks of the same colour in your design, you could work rows of cross stitches by pushing the needle up at 1, down at 2, up at 3, down at 4 and so on, making a row of half stitches from left to right and cross each stitch with another row of half stitches working from right to left (**1f**).

Whether stitching cross stitches individually or in rows, always ensure the top arm of each stitch lies in the same direction. This will result in neat and even stitches. If there is some distance between stitches of the same colour, never be tempted to trail your thread across the back of your work unless you can weave through the back of intervening stitches. It is always better to fasten off a thread and restart further along the fabric to avoid pulling stitches or fabric.

Back stitch

To help define certain areas of a design, back stitch can be used to add outlines and detail. A darker shade of thread, compared to that used for the cross stitching, is usually chosen for adding back stitching and only one strand is required so as not to overpower a design. Back stitch should always be added after all cross stitching has been completed so that the back stitches sit on top of the cross stitches.

On a chart, back stitch is shown as a dark or coloured line around or through each square. To add back stitch, push the needle up at 1, down at 2, up at 3 and down again at 1 (**1g**).

Attaching beads

If attaching beads to your work, this should be done after all cross stitching and back stitching is complete. Each coloured bead to be used in the design will have a corresponding symbol on the chart and will be referenced in the key that accompanies the chart. One square on the chart represents one bead on the fabric.

Thread a beading needle with one strand of embroidery cotton no longer than 20in (508mm) and move the needle to the middle point along the thread. If using many different coloured beads in a close area, or if the beads are light coloured, choose a thread colour that matches the fabric colour. But if all the beads are the same colour, choose a thread that matches either the fabric colour or the bead colour. Begin by weaving through some stitches at the back of your work, close to where your first beaded stitch will be. If this is not possible, leave 1in (25mm) of thread loose at the back of your work and darn it under your stitches when you have finished. The next step is very important as it will anchor your thread in place so that the beads will not work loose. Make two or three small back stitches at the back of the fabric, either in one of your cross stitches or in a block or thread of the fabric and bring the needle through to the front of your work at 1, the point where your first bead will be attached (**2a**).

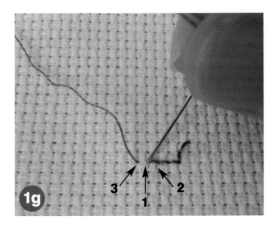

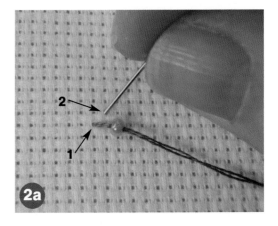

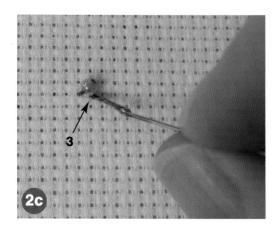

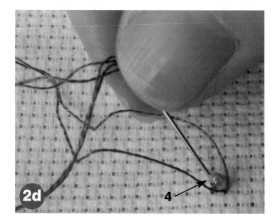

Thread a bead onto the needle and push the needle down at 2 (**2a** and **2b**).

The next stitch will secure the bead. Push the needle up at 3 (**2c**), then split the thread so that one strand lies either side of the bead and push the needle down at 4 (**2d**).

It is a good idea to work in rows – either side to side, or up and down – when attaching the beads. Simply change the colour of bead at each different coloured square so there is no need to finish and restart your thread each time a bead colour changes on the chart.

Finishing a thread

To fasten off a thread, darn about 1in (25mm) through stitches at the back of your work. If finishing off a thread after attaching beads, make two or three small back stitches into the back of some stitches, then darn about 1in (25mm) through stitches at the back of your work. Carefully cut the thread close to your work.

Tweeding

Some of the keys that accompany the projects in this book contain two thread numbers against the one symbol. This means you should thread the needle with one strand of the first colour plus one strand of the second colour listed. This technique is known as 'tweeding' and produces a coloured effect that cannot be achieved by stitching with one cotton colour alone.

Making up a Mini Cushion

Please read through these instructions prior to making up your mini cushion to ensure that you are familiar with all the steps.

1 Place the backing fabric right side up on a flat surface. Then lay your stitched fabric on top of the backing fabric, right side down (**3a**).

If you want to attach a loop for hanging the cushion, or a tassel for extra decoration, then see 'Adding Braids and Tassels' on page 166 before continuing with the instructions.

2 Pin the two pieces together around the outside edges of the design (**3b**).

3 Use strong sewing thread to back stitch the two pieces together around three sides along the edge of the cross stitching and then 1in (25mm) at either end of the fourth side (**3c**), to leave a gap for stuffing.

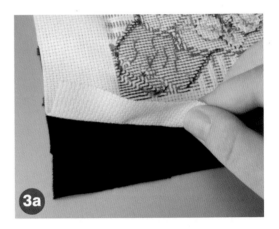

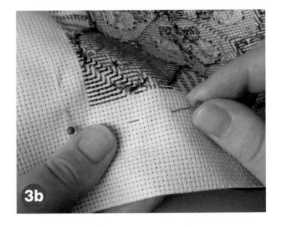

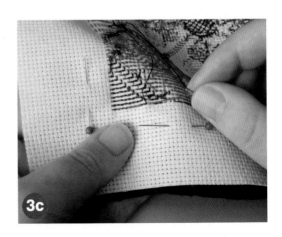

4 Trim all four edges of both the Aida and backing fabric to about four rows from the stitched seam. Then cut across all four corners, taking care not to cut too closely to the stitching, to reduce bulk when turning the mini cushion inside out (**3d**).

5 Carefully turn the mini cushion inside out. You may want to push the blunt end of a pencil into each corner to help turn them out fully. Stuff the cushion with soft filling, being sure to fill the corners firmly. As the mini cushion is small, take care not to over-fill it, because this may spoil the finished result (**3e**).

6 Neatly oversew the opening with strong sewing thread to close up the gap. You now have a beautiful mini cushion to admire and treasure (**3f**).

Adding Braids and Tassels

If you want to hang your mini cushion on a wall you will need to add a loop to it before making up the finished piece. You may also want to add a tassel to hang down from the bottom of the mini cushion. The following steps will show you how, but do take your time as they can be quite tricky.

1 Fold a length of braid (or cord or ribbon) in half (the length will depend on how far you wish the mini cushion to hang down). Lay the braid on top of your stitching so that the two ends of the braid are outside the top corner of the design. The rest of the braid should be curled up on top of the stitching (**4a**).

2 To add a tassel at the opposite corner of the design, lay the tassel on top of the stitching so that the top end is outside the corner of the design. Lay your backing fabric right side down over the cross stitch design, sandwiching the braid and tassel in between. You should now follow the 'Making up a Mini Cushion' instructions on page 164, from step 2 onwards, taking care to catch only the ends of the loop and tassel in the seam (**4b**).

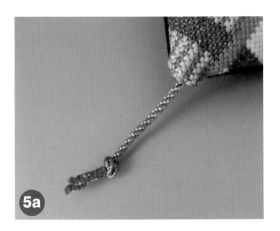

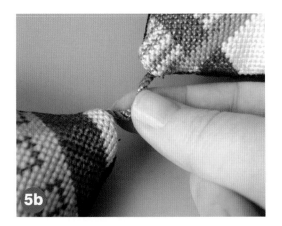

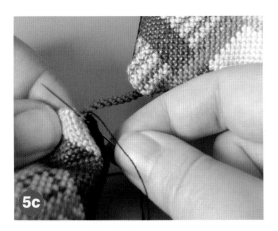

The Taste of India mini cushion on page 143 features an even smaller cushion, which has been added to the bottom corner of the main design. You may want to incorporate a smaller cushion in your other designs and the following instructions will show you how.

1 To make up the larger of the two cushions, sandwich the loop of braid at the top corner for hanging. Sandwich a 3in (76mm) length of braid at the opposite corner, so that when the cushion is turned right side out, 2in (50mm) of braid is hanging out (**5a**).

2 For the smaller cushion, sandwich the tassel at the bottom corner between the stitched Aida and the backing fabric and instead of leaving a gap in one side for turning the cushion inside out, leave the top corner open. Once the larger cushion is complete and the smaller cushion has been filled with stuffing, push 1in (25mm) of the braid from the larger cushion into the opening of the smaller cushion (**5b**).

3 Carefully sew the gap closed, ensuring it is securely stitched to the braid so that the two cushions are attached together (**5c**).

Adding a Beaded Edging

Some of the mini cushions in this book have been given a beaded edging. This finish can be added to any or all of the mini cushions and although it can be a time-consuming technique, the completed effect looks lovely and is well worth the time spent on it.

Whereas seed beads are used within areas of a design, it is better to use rocailles beads for the edging. These have slightly larger holes than seed beads, which are ideal because the technique involves the needle being passed through each bead twice. Having said that, there is no reason why seed beads can not be used for this technique, but you will need to take extra care when threading the needle back through the beads.

1 Thread your needle with a length of sewing thread and tie a small knot in the end. Then pass the needle through the Aida along the seam of the mini cushion and make a few tiny back stitches to secure the thread (**6a**).

2 Thread five beads onto the needle (using a bead colour that matches the cross stitches), plus one bead in a 'master' colour which will act as the tip of each tiny tassel. White has been used as the master colour in the designs in this book but the choice is yours (**6b**).

3 Pass the needle back through the first five beads that were threaded, taking care not to pierce the sewing thread with your needle (**6c**).

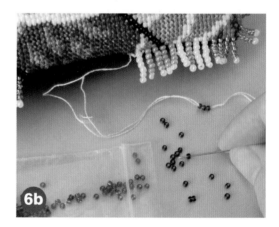

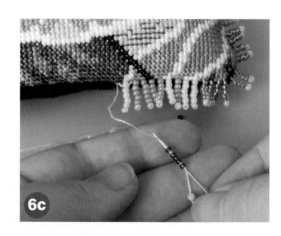

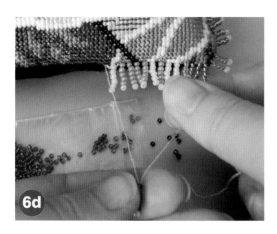

6d

6e

4 Lightly hold the row of beads and pull the needle so that the beads are drawn toward the seam of the cushion (**6d**).

5 Pass the needle through the Aida fabric along the seam of the cushion (**6e**).

6 Repeat steps 2–5 all around the edge of the cushion, using the Aida blocks as a guide for positioning the rows of beads. It is best to miss alternate blocks in the Aida fabric as each beaded tassel will then have a regular space in between.

7 To fasten off the thread, make several small back stitches on the same spot along the seam, then push the needle into the cushion, coming out through the front of the design a short way from the edge. Gently pull the thread and snip it close to the fabric. This end will then sink into the cushion filling.

Making up a Greetings Card

1 Open out the two-fold card and place it face down on a flat surface. Place strips of double-sided sticky tape around all four edges of the aperture and along the left, top and bottom edges of the left hand piece of the card (**7a**).

2 Peel away the backing strips from the tape around the four edges of the aperture (**7b**).

3 Trim the Aida fabric around each edge, four rows away from the edge of the design and lay the design face up on a flat surface. Turn the card over (right side up) and position it over the design so that the design is centred within the aperture. Press the card down onto the fabric (**7c**).

7a

7b

7c

4 Turn the card over so that it is placed face down. Peel away the backing strips from the remaining three pieces of tape (**7d**).

5 Fold over the left-hand flap onto the back of the stitching and press down to secure in place (**7e**).

6 You now have a beautiful card to give or to keep (**7f**).

Blank Chart Template

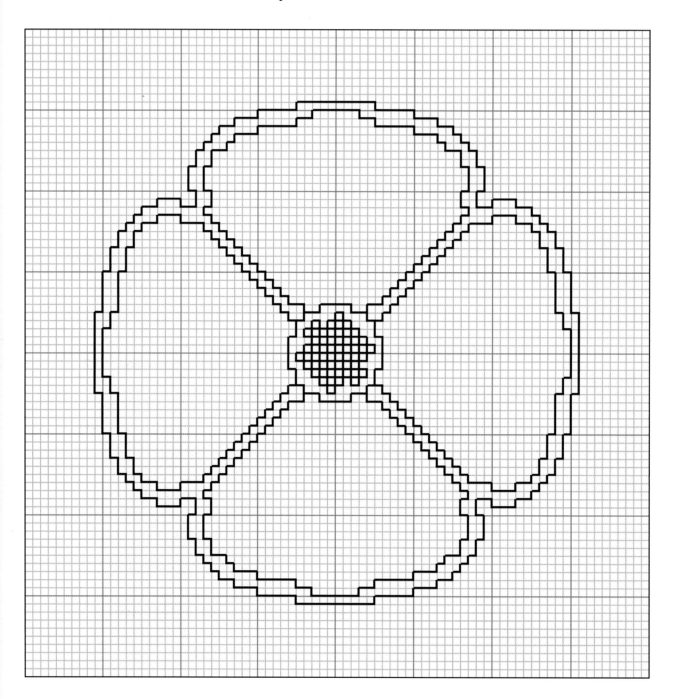

Suppliers

Threads, fabrics, beads

DMC
UK
DMC Creative World Ltd
62 Pullman Road
Wigston
Leicestershire LE18 2DY
+44 (0) 116 281 1040
www.dmc.com

USA
The DMC Corporation
Port Kearny Building
10 South Kearny
NJ 07032
+1 (0) 973 344 0299

AUSTRALIA
DMC Needlecraft Pty Ltd
PO Box 317
Earlwood
NSW 2206
+61 (0) 2 9559 3088

Coats (Anchor Threads)
UK
Coats Crafts UK
PO Box 22
McMullen Road
Darlington
Co. Durham DL1 1YQ
+44 (0) 1325 394 394
www.coatscrafts.co.uk

William Briggs
Unit 52 Halliwell Ind Estate
Rossini Street
Bolton
Lancs BL1 8DL
+44 (0) 1204 599 100

USA
Coats North America
4135 South Stream Blvd.
Charlotte, NC 28217
+1 704 329 5800
www.coatscna.com

AUSTRALIA
Coats Australian Pty Ltd
125 Station Road
Seven Hills
New South Wales 2147
+61 2 9838 5200

Madeira Threads
UK
Madeira Threads (UK) Ltd
Thirsk Industrial Park
York Road
Thirsk
North Yorkshire Y07 3BX
+44 (0) 18 45 52 48 80
www.madeira.co.uk

AUSTRALIA
Penguin Threads Pty Ltd
35 Mount Street,
Prahran, 3181 Victoria
+61 3 9529 4400
www.penguin-threads.com.au

Fabric, beads and threads

Willow Fabrics
95 Town Lane
Mobberley
Knutsford
Cheshire WA16 7HH
UK
0800 056 7811
+44 (0)1565 87 22 25
www.willowfabrics.com

Two-fold greetings cards

Craft Creations Ltd
Ingersoll House,
Delamare Road,
Cheshunt,
Hertfordshire EN8 9HD
UK
+44 (0) 1992 781900
www.craftcreations.co.uk

Beads

Mill Hill Beads
N162 Hwy 35
Stoddard, WI 54658
USA
www.millhillbeads.com

Perivale-Gütermann Ltd.
Bullsbrook Road
Hayes
Middlesex UB4 OJR
UK
+44 (0) 20 8589 1600
www.guetermann.com

About the Author

Sheena Rogers has enjoyed painting and drawing for many years and took up cross stitch in 1990, as part of her Art & Design A level. She began designing soon afterwards and now combines her cross stitch and drawing skills in designing new patterns. She also designs tapestries and enjoys experimenting with other materials, and her interest in craft, particularly cross stitch and embroidery, extends to their history and development.

For the past two years she has stitched a series of ten cross stitch designs by another designer and her work has featured in *The World of Cross Stitching* magazine. This is her second book for GMC Publications. Her first, *Cross Stitch in Colour*, was published in 1996.

Index

WITHDRAWN

Guild of Master Craftsman Publications

Castle Place, 166 High Street, Lewes

East Sussex BN7 1XU, United Kingdom

Tel: 01273 488005 Fax: 01273 402866

Website: www.thegmcgroup.com

Contact us for a complete catalogue, or visit our website.

Orders by credit card are accepted.